READING STREET

Sleuth

COMMON CORE

PEARSON

Glenview, Illinois
Boston, Massachusetts
Chandler, Arizona
Upper Saddle River, New Jersey

Acknowledgments appear on page 78, which constitutes an extension of this copyright page.

ISBN-13: 978-0-328-73057-5
ISBN-10: 0-328-73057-2
9 10 V003 16 15 14

Contents

From: The Super Sleuths

Subject: Mysteries

Dear Sleuthhound,

All we have are some clues. Where will they lead? How will the clues fit together? We need your help to answer some really big questions. Use all the tools that sleuths can use to collect evidence and make a case to justify your thinking. Be curious. Ask questions that will take you in new directions. Look closely and see what others might not see. This book is full of mysteries to help you practice all your sleuth skills. Keep these Super Sleuth Steps in your pocket to help you.

We're depending on you!

SUPER SLEUTH STEPS

Gather Evidence

- Look back through the text and the images for details others might miss.

- Record the facts. No successful sleuth expects to remember everything without taking notes.

- Organize the evidence. See how the pieces fit together.

Ask Questions

- A great question can make all the difference! Perhaps nobody else may think to ask it.

- Be curious. You may learn something new and exciting!

Make Your Case

- Look at all the evidence and draw a conclusion. Take a stand!

- Put the evidence together to make a convincing argument. Include a clearly stated position or conclusion that is based on solid evidence. Present your case with confidence!

Prove It!

- When it's time to wrap up the case, take what you have learned and amaze everyone.

- A Super Sleuth can work alone or as part of a team. Remember, sleuths can learn something from everyone.

Unit 1
Turning Points

Hello, Sleuthhounds!

In this unit, you will be looking for evidence about discoveries from new people or in new places. Here are some sleuth tips to help you. Good luck!

Sleuth Tips

Gather Evidence

Where do sleuths find evidence?

- Sleuths find evidence in the text and images. They look for details that others might miss.
- Sleuths also infer information based on their own experiences.

Ask Questions

What types of questions do sleuths ask?

- Sleuths ask who, what, when, where, why, and how questions.
- Sleuths think carefully about what information is missing, and they ask questions that will reveal hidden evidence.

Make Your Case

How do sleuths reach a conclusion?

- Sleuths look carefully at the evidence they have gathered. They classify, determine sequence, compare, contrast, or look for causes and effects.
- Sleuths know that a case based on opinion isn't as strong as a case based on facts and solid evidence.

Prove It!

How do sleuths prove they have learned something new?

- Sleuths think about what they learned from others and from asking additional questions.
- Sleuths reread what they have written to be certain it is clear and free of errors.

IN HARMONY

Come one! Come all! The circus is in town. In St. Louis, Missouri, it's Circus Harmony that is under the big top. You don't want to miss this circus! This circus isn't just about entertaining. More importantly, it teaches harmony and peace among children from all different kinds of backgrounds. Circus Harmony is for children of different ages, races, genders, and religions.

Since 2001, Circus Harmony has been teaching children all kinds of circus tricks. Children don't just learn to juggle or build human pyramids here. They also learn to work together as they perform circus acts. They learn to cooperate and to connect to each other no matter where they are from, what color their skin is, or if their families are rich or poor. Circus Harmony teaches children skills that they use here at the circus, but also in life. Children learn how to take control over their own bodies, minds, and emotions. They also learn that it is more important to focus on the similarities among them than to point out the differences. Can you believe it? Children learn all these important skills as they practice performing circus acts!

Circus Harmony performs circus acts in front of hundreds of people every year. Circus Harmony has even joined Ringling Brothers and Barnum and Bailey Circus when in St. Louis. Circus Harmony is definitely an act that deserves a standing ovation!

SLEUTH WORK

Gather Evidence What words does the author use to give her opinion about Circus Harmony? Write these words in a list.

Ask Questions What questions might parents ask Circus Harmony before signing their children up to participate in this circus? Write at least three questions.

Make Your Case Is Circus Harmony more similar to or more different from a regular circus? Give evidence from the text to support your answer.

Alano Español:
A Dying Breed?

More than 1,600 years ago, the country we now call Spain was invaded by the Alans. The Alans came from thousands of miles away, near what is now the country of Iran. Invaders from other countries were driving them out of their homeland. The Alans traveled across Europe, bringing their dogs with them. As Spanish explorers traveled to new lands, they also took these dogs with them.

This ancient dog breed is known as Alano Español, which means "Spanish bulldog." These dogs are very large. They have big, square heads, like the head of a bulldog. The dogs' front legs are very strong, and they have large paws. Their fur is short and thick, allowing them to live outside in any kind of weather. They do not drool or slobber, and they rarely bark. These dogs follow commands by their owners and are loyal, protecting their owners and their property.

The Alans found these big, strong dogs very useful. The dogs could run for long periods of time without getting tired. This helped them herd wild cattle. They also helped their owners hunt and fight in wars.

Alanos Españoles are used to herd cattle.

Because Spanish bulldogs had strong jaws and could hold on to wild animals, they were invaluable for hunting. These dogs were fierce around strangers but very loving with the people who owned them.

Although the Alano Español could be found in many parts of Europe at one time, this breed seemed to have died out everywhere except in Spain. Today, however, these bulldogs have found their way to North America. Dog breeders have imported these unusual dogs for dog owners who are looking for a rare breed. Spanish bulldogs continue to be hardworking dogs for their owners. These are loyal dogs that still herd cattle and hunt with their owners.

Sleuth Work

Gather Evidence Which words in the article describe what an Alano Español looks like? Make a list of these words.

Ask Questions If you wanted to get an Alano Español for a pet, what questions would you ask about the dog before you decided to buy one? Write at least three questions.

Make Your Case Should explorers have taken their pets with them when they traveled to new lands, or should they have left their pets at home? Give evidence to support your answer.

SPACE CAMP EXPLORERS

Have you ever looked up at the sky and wondered what it is like in space? Imagine putting on a spacesuit and blasting off on a spaceship to find out. While this may seem like a far-off dream, the National Aeronautics and Space Administration (NASA) gives kids a chance to see what it is like to explore space.

Camp Kennedy Space Center is a weeklong camp that is offered each summer. It is held at the Kennedy Space Center in Florida. Campers from ages eight to fourteen enjoy space-related fun and adventure.

While at the camp, campers see and feel what it is like to train to be an astronaut and explore the universe. For example, they work in teams to study the future of space travel. They design space exploration vehicles and places to live in space. They meet real astronauts and ask them questions about their work.

Campers experience the speed with which space vehicles travel. They also get to see what it is like to be weightless. After all, there is no gravity in space to keep astronauts on the ground! Space campers get a small taste of this.

Perhaps the most thrilling part of space camp is stepping into the Space Shuttle Launch Simulator. The simulator is a towering six-story building. It looks just like the space shuttle launch site at Cape Canaveral, Florida. Inside, astronauts walk campers through the steps of a space shuttle launch, right up to the final countdown. Three, two, one, blast off! Campers experience sound and lighting effects that are similar to a real space shuttle launch. It is a very exciting event!

Campers at Camp Kennedy Space Center have a lot of fun, and they learn a lot too. Each year, NASA hopes the camp experience will inspire a few campers to become astronauts and explore space.

Sleuth Work

Gather Evidence What evidence can you find that tells you how the author feels about space camp? Write two details.

Ask Questions If you were to go to space camp, what questions might you ask the astronauts there? Write three interesting questions.

Make Your Case Which would you enjoy attending more: space camp or another type of specialty camp such as music or sports camp? State your reasons in a paragraph and support your opinion with evidence from the text.

The Meeting

It was a typical night in New Mexico—cool, arid air and stars shining bright in the sky. Only one thing made this night different from the others. A meeting was going on and all the desert creatures were there.

The Black Widow was the first to speak. "The desert can be a scary place so it is essential that we are all able to defend ourselves. I can spin a sticky web. If I'm disturbed, I can rush forward and inject poisonous venom into the disturber. I can even suck out the liquid contents of my victim's body. What can the rest of you do to defend yourselves?"

The rest of the desert creatures thought about what they each could do to defend themselves.

"Everyone's afraid of monsters!" stated Gila Monster proudly. "Instead of basking in the sun, I'll sneak up on an intruder. Then, with one deadly bite, they'll be done for."

Fire Ant spoke up next. "When attacked, I call in my army of ants. With little warning, we swarm the intruders, and then we bite them and sting them! We might be little, but we are mighty aggressive!"

Then Rattlesnake spoke up, although he really preferred to keep to himself. He shared that, when threatened, he slithers up and sinks his sharp fangs into intruders that come too close.

Tarantula added to the discussion. "Unlike other spiders, I don't trap my prey in sticky webs. Instead I use my large legs to grab them and then turn on them with my sharp fangs, injecting poison."

Tarantula then turned to Conenose bug and suggested that his famous deadly kiss is likely his best defense.

African Honeybee buzzed into the meeting, just arriving back home from an extended safari. The small bee took center stage. "My colony is well trained in defense," buzzed African Honeybee. "We have poisoned more enemies than all of you combined. It's our pleasure to rid these foothills of any intruders."

The meeting ended with everyone knowing they could do their part in defending themselves. Then they all had a restful and safe sleep.

Sleuth Work

Gather Evidence Choose one creature from the story. Make a list of details the author includes that tell you about the characteristics of that desert creature.

Ask Questions Which animal would you like to learn more about? Write three questions you'd like to answer about that creature.

Make Your Case Which animal do you think would be the most successful defending itself? Write a paragraph and give evidence that supports your opinion.

Down the Wrong Path

Preparations for our family vacation were under way, and our house was bustling. Dad was securing camping gear to the roof of the car, and Mom was packing a cooler with food. My sister, Maggie, was fidgeting with the compass she got for her birthday, but I was just sitting on the couch dreading our trip to Yosemite National Park.

Once on the road, Dad reviewed every detail of the itinerary, and at every turn, Maggie announced the direction on her compass.

When we arrived at Yosemite, Mom passed out sandwiches. "Be sure to leave not even a crumb," Mom warned. "There are hungry black bears around here."

"Great," I grumbled.

After lunch, we set out on the Valley Floor Loop, which is a thirteen-mile trail, but we were only walking half the loop. When we came to a fork in the trail about a mile into the hike, Mom asked, "Which way?"

Maggie studied her compass while Dad consulted the map. "That way!" they exclaimed in unison, pointing to the left.

An hour went by and then another; the sun sank to the west. "Dad, are we there yet?" I asked.

"Not sure, kiddo." He frowned.

"We must've walked more than six miles by now," Mom said. "Let's take a break." We rested on a log while Dad examined the map and compass.

"Maggie," Dad started, "which direction did the compass point back at the fork?"

"I don't remember," she said.

"Great," I grumbled. I refused to spend the night in the wilderness with my family and those bears. "Let me take a look," I said. I had aced my geography class, so hopefully I could get us out of this sticky situation.

I spread the map on the ground and turned it so that north on the map matched north on the compass. We had just passed El Capitan, so I located that on the map. "We are following the whole loop trail, not the half loop," I explained, "so we need to turn back." I traced the path on the map with my finger.

As we approached camp, Mom exclaimed, "Max, you did it!" I smiled a little shyly. I think Mom was glad we didn't have to sleep with the hungry bears.

That night we roasted marshmallows on the campfire. Maybe camping isn't so bad after all.

Sleuth Work

Gather Evidence Max dreaded the trip to Yosemite. What evidence supports this idea? Make a list.

Ask Questions What questions might you ask Max to learn why he was dreading the trip to Yosemite? Write two questions you would ask him.

Make Your Case Would Yosemite be a place you might enjoy visiting? Give evidence from the text to explain your opinion.

Unit 2
Teamwork

Hi, Sleuthhounds!
In this unit, you will be looking for clues about all sorts of teams. Here are some sleuth tips to help you. Here we go!

Sleuth Tips

Gather Evidence

Why do sleuths reread?

- Sleuths know that something can be missed the first time.
- Sleuths look for details when they reread. They keep looking for clues!

Ask Questions

What makes a great question?

- Sleuths ask great questions to help them learn something. Great questions are clear and focused on the topic.
- Sleuths ask questions that will make everyone think more deeply.

Make Your Case

How do sleuths make a clear case?

- Sleuths clearly state what they believe when making a case.
- Sleuths give reasons that are based on what they have learned. They lay out the evidence step by step.

Prove It!

What do sleuths do when they work with other sleuths?

- Sleuths share the evidence they have gathered.
- Sleuths share the work and the fun. They make certain everyone participates.

Winning GOLD

Mike loved swimming and basketball. During summer, he'd race any kid who challenged him in the pool, and he spent hours playing basketball with his older brothers. Mike especially attacked the basketball court with lots of energy and enthusiasm—that is until something didn't go his way. Then he stomped off the court.

At school, Mike tried out for the basketball team and made it. Mike was always the first one to the gym. He couldn't wait to run around the court and dribble the ball. He loved shooting from the free-throw line too.

Coach Sikes was impressed by Mike's enthusiasm and how fast he ran up and down the court. However, in a game, Mike lost focus easily. He got distracted when players bumped into him, and he got angry when things didn't go his way. This concerned the coach. He knew Mike had speed, but he had difficulty being a team player.

Coach Sikes talked with Mike's dad. Mike's dad told the coach that Mike was a boy filled with energy, but he often let the excitement of a game hurt his focus.

As Coach Sikes worked with Mike, he learned how much Mike loved to swim too. He encouraged Mike to try out for the local swim team. Coach Sikes knew that swimming would allow Mike to use his speed and enthusiasm, and he'd be able to focus much more easily with no one bumping him as he swam.

Mike made the swim team and was the fastest swimmer in his grade. As he developed the ability to focus on what he needed to do in the pool, his behavior improved on the basketball court. Mike's speed and ability brought home the gold for his team more than once!

Sleuth Work

Gather Evidence How did the events on the basketball court lead to Mike winning gold as a swimmer? Find clues in the text to explain your answer.

Ask Questions Write two questions Coach Sikes might ask Mike's dad to help him better coach Mike.

Make Your Case Do you think a person's participation in a solo sport like swimming can improve his or her performance in a team sport like basketball? Make a list of reasons to support your answer.

❖ THE ❖
Metro City News

Helen Ellison began her day as she did every day. She picked up the paper from her front porch and read it at the breakfast table. Ms. Ellison was the managing editor of the daily *Metro City News*.

After she finished reading the paper, she went to work downtown. Inside the tall newspaper building were rooms full of desks, computers, and telephones.

Today Ms. Ellison's son, Henry, was going to work with her. Henry loved seeing how the newspaper was made. Fascinated by the hustle and bustle, he watched reporters work furiously to make tight deadlines and get their stories ready for the next day's paper.

"Now, Henry," reminded his mother, "Mr. Townsend can't talk baseball today. He has an important deadline to make."

"OK, Mom," Henry said, as he wandered past a row of reporters who were making calls and typing up stories on the computer.

Henry stopped to visit with Juan, one of the newspaper's photographers. Juan took pictures to coordinate with news stories, and like all newspaper photographers, he hoped his picture would be picked for the front page.

"Hey, Henry, look for my picture on the front page tomorrow," Juan said. "I got an incredible shot of that big warehouse fire this morning!" Henry gave him a high five.

Henry passed by a row of copy editors. He didn't bother them as they were focused on making sure stories were well written and accurate. The copy editors checked every word and sentence carefully, looking for spelling mistakes or missing punctuation. Henry knew he would be horrible at that job. Spelling wasn't his best subject.

Next Henry stopped in the design department. Here he could see the paper being laid out on the computer. Designers made sure all news stories, photos, and ads fit on each page. They also worked on the Internet version of the newspaper that people read on their computers and smartphones.

Henry ended his day in his favorite part of the building: the printing press area. Huge rolls of paper were loaded onto enormous printing machines. The metal printing plates were inked up and long sheets of paper rolled under the inked plates. Finally, the long sheets were cut apart into smaller pages and folded together into a paper.

As Henry headed back to his mom's office, he pulled a fresh paper off a stack of newly printed papers. He loved getting a newspaper hot off the presses!

SLEUTH WORK

Gather Evidence What evidence can you find to support the idea that it takes many people working together to put out a newspaper?

Ask Questions If you were a reporter covering a news story, what questions would you ask your editor before you went out to gather facts?

Make Your Case Do you think there will still be paper newspapers when you are an adult, or will all the information only be available electronically? Support your predictions with three convincing reasons.

PLAYING SPORTS and Giving Back

Professional sports teams make their fans cheer by winning games and championships. Winning is not just about scoring touchdowns, making baskets, and hitting homeruns, though. Many teams and players are winners because they help their communities. They know they are in a unique position to make a difference. Most are very happy to lend their names, time, autographed items, and money to help raise funds and awareness about important causes.

Some sports organizations choose certain charities to support. For example, Major League Baseball® has chosen Boys & Girls Clubs of America   as its official charity. Together, these two organizations help children learn to deal with barriers and challenges in their lives. Boys and girls are also taught about sportsmanship, responsibility, and team spirit.

The National Hockey League® focuses its charity work on fighting cancer. In 1998, the league, along with the National Hockey League Players' Association™ started a program called Hockey Fights Cancer™. In 1999, the two organizations started the Hockey's All-Star Kids Foundation™. This program connects the hockey community with young people who have cancer and other serious diseases.

There are some causes many sports teams help support. One such cause is childhood obesity. When a child is obese, he or she weighs more than is healthy. This can lead to serious problems later in life. Today, more and more children are obese. Sports teams want to help children learn to take better care of their bodies. The Chicago Fire®, Denver Nuggets®, and Atlanta Falcons® are just a few of the teams that help support programs to teach children about good nutrition and the importance of regular exercise. The National Football League® started NFL PLAY 60™. This program encourages young football fans to be active for at least sixty minutes every day.

The Sports Philanthropy Project is an organization that helps sports teams give back to communities. It also keeps track of what teams and players are doing to make a difference. Do you want to know what your favorite teams and players are doing? Visit their Web sites to find out.

Sleuth Work

Ask Questions What questions might you ask a player about giving back to his or her community? Write three questions.

Gather Evidence What types of causes are important to sports teams and players? Give examples from the text.

Make Your Case Do you think sports players should have to give back to their communities? State your reasons in a paragraph.

Raising Puppies for Others

Do you love puppies? Have you ever thought of becoming a Puppy Raiser? Puppy Raisers raise puppies to be Seeing Eye dogs.

A Seeing Eye dog is a dog that helps people who are visually challenged or who have other serious visual disabilities. Seeing Eye dogs, or guide dogs, help people get around in their daily lives. When they have the right training, these dogs can guide their masters around busy sidewalks and streets and through crowded malls and airports.

As a Puppy Raiser, your family gets a puppy when it's young, about eight weeks old. Your job is to foster the puppy, giving it a home until it's about eighteen months old. During that time, you must socialize the puppy, or take the puppy almost everywhere with you. The puppy needs to get used to being around people in many different situations, especially noisy and busy places.

As a Puppy Raiser, you must take the puppy to obedience classes. At the classes, the puppy learns how to obey commands like *sit*, *stay*, and *come*. The puppy learns to lie down on command and walk on a leash too. Your job as a Puppy Raiser is to practice with the puppy until it masters all of these skills.

After about a year and a half, the puppy heads off to more training where it learns to be a Seeing Eye dog. This training will get the dog ready for a new owner—a visually challenged person who will depend on that dog to help make life easier.

So do you want to be a Puppy Raiser? First, your parents must fill out an application and go through an interview. If your family is accepted into the program, you receive a puppy plus all the things your puppy needs, including food, a dish, a leash, and more. Then you can enjoy training the new puppy. When the puppy moves on to do its job, you can always foster another puppy!

Sleuth Work

Gather Evidence What evidence can you find that training a Seeing Eye dog helps people? Write two details that you find.

Ask Questions If you were to consider becoming a Puppy Raiser, what are two questions you might ask about the program? Write your questions.

Make Your Case Do you think that being a Puppy Raiser is more fun or more work? Write two reasons that support your opinion.

The First Lady's Job

Almost every President of the United States has been married. The President has a title, but what about the President's spouse? The wife of the President is called the First Lady. The role of the First Lady has changed over time. At one time, the First Lady was responsible for planning and hosting social events at the White House and accompanying the President to ceremonies. However, over the years, these women decided to make a larger impact while in the White House.

First Ladies have advocated, or spoken up for, a variety of causes, such as volunteering and literacy. The First Lady has an office in the East Wing of the White House. She also has aides, interns, and volunteers who work with her.

First Ladies have helped to raise awareness about different topics and causes that they support. Lady Bird Johnson, wife of Lyndon B. Johnson, was passionate about nature. She started a beautification program, which led to the planting of many trees and flowers in Washington, D.C. Barbara Bush, wife of George H. W. Bush, promoted the importance of reading and writing. She also encouraged people to become volunteers and help those who were sick or homeless. Michelle Obama, wife of Barack Obama, decided to use her

Lady Bird Johnson

Barbara Bush

time in the White House to gather support for the families of our nation's military and to encourage children to get more exercise and eat more healthful foods.

After their husbands left office, most First Ladies left Washington, D.C., and returned to a fairly private life. Hillary Clinton, the wife of Bill Clinton, was different. In fact, she is the only First Lady to have been elected to public office. After leaving the White House, she was elected to the U.S. Senate from the state of New York. She later became the nation's Secretary of State.

In 2007, Hillary Clinton ran for President. She became one of the few women in the history of the United States to have done so. Although she did not win, one day there may be a woman as President of the United States. There may be a First Gentleman who accompanies her to the White House. Do you think the First Gentleman's job might be different from the First Lady's job?

Michelle Obama

Hillary Clinton

Sleuth Work

Gather Evidence Write a brief description of the work of First Ladies. Use details from the text.

Ask Questions Suppose a former First Lady was going to visit your class. Write three questions you would like to ask her about her job as First Lady.

Make Your Case Do you think a First Lady or First Gentleman should be given a salary? Justify your opinion with facts from this text or other research.

Unit 3
Patterns in Nature

Hello there, Sleuthhounds!

In this unit, you will be looking for clues about patterns found in nature. Here are some sleuth tips to help you. All the best!

Sleuth Tips

Gather Evidence

How do sleuths get clues from images?

- Sleuths use pictures, charts, maps, and other visuals to learn even more about a topic.
- Sleuths connect what they read with the additional information from the images.

Ask Questions

Why are sleuths so curious?

- Sleuths know that they can't get answers without asking questions.
- Sleuths love to find the unexpected. They are always ready to follow clues that may lead them in a new direction.

Make Your Case

Why don't all sleuths agree on the answers?

- Sleuths find different evidence. They may also put the evidence together differently to reach another conclusion.
- Sleuths know we all have different backgrounds and experiences. That means that each sleuth might draw a different conclusion.

Prove It!

How can sleuths show what they have learned creatively?

- Sleuths explain their ideas in unique ways.
  They might use images to help others picture what they have in their minds.
- Sleuths try to use powerful and persuasive language. They want to keep the attention of the reader or listener.

Do you need to wear a jacket today? Is it important to bring an umbrella with you? Meteorologists help us answer those weather questions, but meteorologists are more than just the people on TV telling us what the weather is going to be like today.

Meteorologists are scientists. They go to school to learn all about the weather and what creates it. Meteorologists depend on science and tools to help explain the Earth's atmosphere and how that atmosphere impacts our weather.

Predicting the weather is a big part of being a meteorologist. Today, meteorologists depend on technology and people around the world to help predict the weather. Meteorologists get help from weather observers all over the world.

Weather observers are very important to our local meteorologists. These observers, located around the globe, make measurements every day at nearly 10,000 different weather stations. In addition, thousands of ships at sea record the weather. More than 500 weather stations release weather balloons to measure temperature, wind, and other things that occur above the Earth's surface. All of this data is collected and examined. Then the data is used to make weather predictions.

Some meteorologists do more than predict the weather. These scientists work in atmospheric research, which means they study the atmosphere and how it affects people, animals, oceans, and

Average Monthly High Temperature in Chicago, IL

Jan	Feb	Mar	Apr	May	Jun	Jul	Aug	Sep	Oct	Nov	Dec

land. Meteorologists work hard at studying the impact of global climate change on our environment. They also study how pollution affects our weather, what causes hurricanes to form, and what causes droughts.

Being a meteorologist is an important job! Meteorologists help us stay safe during dangerous weather. They work with city managers to plan the number of snowplows that will be needed during winter storms. They help farmers understand how to farm during difficult weather patterns. They provide information to power companies to help them meet energy needs during hot or cold spells. They even help sporting event organizers predict whether a game can go on after a rain delay.

So the next time you watch a meteorologist on TV, keep in mind that the two-minute weather forecast is based on hours of research. Meteorologists don't *always* get their predictions right, but thanks to lots of teamwork, they are often pretty accurate.

Sleuth Work

Gather Evidence What clues can you find that tell you the author's opinion about meteorologists? Write these words in a list.

Ask Questions Write three questions to ask someone in your class using the information on the graph.

Make Your Case Would you be a good meteorologist? Write your opinion and the reasons for your opinion. Use information from the text about the skills a meteorologist needs to have.

The Amazing Migration of the Arctic Tern

The Arctic tern is a small bird that makes a big trip each year. In fact, it makes the longest migration of any bird in the world. Every spring, the Arctic tern lays its eggs and raises its hatchlings on the rocky ground near the North Pole. Every fall it flies to the South Pole, where it spends months on the ice of Antarctica. That's a round trip of more than 21,750 miles (35,000 kilometers) each year!

Arctic terns are fancy fliers but they are not fancy birds. They are related to gulls. Arctic terns are about 12 to 15 inches (30 to 38 centimeters) long. They have a cap of white feathers on their heads and a long, forked tail. They also have webbed feet, which help them swim when they dive into the water to catch fish.

Most birds that migrate are trying to find the best places to live at different times of the year. Birds that live where the seasons change are usually flying to a place where it will be easier for them to find food and shelter. Birds that live where it is warm all year, such as Africa, will migrate to different areas depending on when the rainy season or the dry season comes.

Migrating birds use natural landmarks, such as bodies of water and landmasses, to help them find their way as they travel. Scientists also believe birds are born with some sense of when it's time to migrate and where they need to go. When Arctic terns migrate, they leave their hatching grounds in the north and travel south along the coast toward Antarctica.

Arctic terns have two summers each year. They are able to enjoy the long summer days of the Arctic as well as the long summer days of Antarctica. Arctic terns experience more daylight hours than any other animal on Earth. In June, July, and August, Arctic terns live in the Arctic. Then they spend three months flying south. In December, January, and February they live in the Antarctic. This pattern repeats itself over and over again. That's a bird that really "goes the distance!"

Sleuth Work

Gather Evidence Write down evidence from the article that tells what kind of weather the Arctic tern prefers.

Ask Questions Write three interesting questions you would ask an expert in bird migration using information from the text and images. Where would you look to learn the answer to one of those questions?

Make Your Case Do you think scientists should spend time and money studying the migration patterns of animals? Write a paragraph that explains your opinion. Give two pieces of evidence to support your opinion.

A STORY OF THE SEASONS

One day Persephone (pur-SEF-uh-nee) was out for a walk on a warm, beautiful day. She came across a meadow and spotted some beautiful flowers. She decided to wander into the meadow to gather some of the flowers for her mother, Demeter (dih-MEE-tur). Demeter was the goddess of agriculture.

Persephone believed her mother would enjoy seeing how beautiful her creations were. She knew she would have no trouble picking as many flowers as she chose, as Zeus (zoos) was her father. Zeus was the chief god who was in charge of all things. Who would argue with him over some flowers?

As Persephone was gathering her flowers, she became lost in her thoughts. Because of this, she didn't notice as a huge crack opened up in the earth. Then, all at once, Hades (HAY-dees)—the king of the underworld—stood before her admiring her beauty. Before she could react, Hades grabbed Persephone and brought her with him back down to the underworld.

Soon the news of the kidnapping spread to Demeter. She was horrified and immediately started to search for her daughter. She wandered the earth to locate her. In her sorrow, the goddess of agriculture became so focused on finding her daughter that she became uninterested with the harvest or the fruitfulness of the earth. Because of this, the crops withered and died, and it became winter year-round.

Demeter pleaded with Zeus to do something. He finally demanded that Hades set Persephone free to her mother. However, Hades had a demand of his own. Since Persephone had eaten one pomegranate seed during her time in the underworld, she could not be freed completely. She had to spend part of the year with Hades, and the other part she could spend with her mother.

The ancient Greeks believed this is why we have seasons. The time Persephone spends with her mother is during the seasons of spring and summer, when flowers bloom and fruits are plentiful. The time Persephone spends with Hades is fall and winter, when the land is cold and barren.

SLEUTH WORK

Gather Evidence What clues tell you that Demeter was a powerful goddess?

Ask Questions Zeus was the chief god. What questions might you ask him about his responsibilities?

Make Your Case Did Zeus make the best decision by accepting the offer from Hades? Write your opinion and give at least two reasons to support it.

TORNADO SIRENS—
What's the Use?

Did you know that more than twelve hundred tornadoes touched down in the United States in 2010? Sirens are often used to alert people of the possibility of a tornado. However, from my experience growing up in the South, I think that tornado sirens are now obsolete. Tornado sirens have outlived their usefulness.

Obviously, it is important for communities to have ways to warn the public of danger. In the past, bells hung high in towers warned people about bad weather, fires, or wars. When communities began to use electricity in the 1930s, sirens replaced bells as the warning signal.

I grew up listening to the blares of tornado siren tests every Wednesday morning at 10:00. Clear, sunny days in the summer were suddenly interrupted with a deafening tone whirling through the air. I got used to ignoring them. In the South where I grew up, severe thunderstorms are common. We would stand on our porch and watch as the sky turned dark, and then green. If the tornado sirens started to blare, we didn't think much of it. However, we should have been preparing for a tornado! But hearing the sirens was so commonplace that it didn't concern us.

On the other hand, tornado sirens can cause undue panic to people who aren't used to them. Once, a visitor from out of town heard the Wednesday morning test of the sirens. She panicked, sending all of the children inside for shelter. There was not a rain cloud in sight. Such is the power of a tornado siren!

In the 1800s, community leaders believed tornado warnings would cause people to panic. The word *tornado* was even banned from all forecasts! Now, communities expect to be warned about the possibility of tornadoes.

However, there are better ways now to warn people than by using sirens. By the 1960s, radio and television warning systems made the outdoor sirens less useful. Since 1995, the Internet and cell phones have been connecting the public to the best and most accurate weather technology; outdoor sirens are unnecessary.

Cell phones can tell you where the storm is headed and can help you locate the nearest tornado shelter. With a siren, you have only a general warning; you can't tell whether or not you are in danger.

Finally, sirens can cost tens of thousands of dollars. Surely, the money is better spent making sure that accurate emergency information is communicated through televisions, radios, cell phones, and over the Internet.

SLEUTH WORK

Gather Evidence What clues can you find that tell you the author is giving both facts and opinions?

Make Your Case Choose a side. List three convincing reasons for or against spending more government money on tornado warning systems.

Ask Questions Find someone who chose the opposite viewpoint on the spending issue. Ask that person one factual and one opinion question related to tornado warning systems.

Crater Lake

What images come to mind when you think of a volcano? Perhaps you think of molten lava spewing from one, or smoke pouring into the sky and covering the earth with ash. You probably wouldn't think of a fresh lake with the clearest and bluest water, would you?

Thousands of years ago the top of a volcano named Mount Mazama collapsed due to a powerful eruption. This resulted in a crater on top of the now inactive volcano. Lava sealed the bottom of the crater creating a basin. This basin gradually filled with water from rain and snowmelt. This crater is now called Crater Lake.

Nestled high in the Cascade Mountains of Oregon, Crater Lake is one of the deepest lakes in the world. The walls of old Mount Mazama tower above the lake, rising from 500 to 2,000 feet (152 to 610 meters). At its widest point, Crater Lake is about 6 miles (9 kilometers) across.

Crater Lake is known for its blue color. The lake is so blue because it is very deep. In fact, this lake was once called Deep Blue Lake. The water is also nearly pure, which is a reason why the water is clear. Its purity and clarity are due to the fact that no rivers or streams flow into the lake.

If you visit Crater Lake, you will notice two islands: Wizard Island and Phantom Ship. You may also see a mountain hemlock log floating upright in the lake. What's so special about this log? It's known as the "Old Man" of Crater Lake, and it has been floating around the lake for over 100 years!

Today Crater Lake sits in Crater Lake National Park. Thanks to William Gladstone Steel, the lake and the surrounding area have been protected and preserved as a national park since 1902. Tourists can enjoy camping, fishing, and hiking during the warm months. However, from October to June, the park is buried under snow. No matter the season, Crater Lake is considered a place of great beauty.

Sleuth Work

Gather Evidence How did Crater Lake form? Use evidence from the text to make a list of the events in the order in which they happened.

Ask Questions Write three questions you would ask a park ranger at Crater Lake National Park.

Make Your Case Should the park service be allowed to give boat tours of Crater Lake or should the lake be off-limits to all boats? Write a paragraph and include three convincing reasons to support your opinion.

Unit 4
Puzzles and Mysteries

Hi, Sleuthhounds!
In this unit, you will be looking for clues about some cool mysteries. Here are some sleuth tips to help you. Enjoy the adventure!

Sleuth Tips

Gather Evidence

How do sleuths remember clues?

- Sleuths know that everyone forgets. They take notes and write down the details.
- Sleuths use many ways to help remember what is important. They make lists, draw diagrams, and create charts.

Ask Questions

Why do sleuths ask questions?

- Sleuths need to ask questions to gather facts and evidence. These questions can help find answers.
- Sleuths know that good questions can lead to interesting answers.

Make Your Case

How do sleuths disagree with other sleuths?

- Sleuths don't expect everyone to agree. They are curious about other ideas.
- Sleuths ask questions to help them understand how others may have come to a different conclusion.

Prove It!

What do sleuths think about before showing what they have learned?

- Sleuths look back at their notes. They focus on what is most important to share.
- Sleuths try to find the most clear and convincing way to show what they know. They often make an outline.

Don't Believe What You See

Have you ever felt like your eyes were playing tricks on you? You might have been experiencing an optical illusion. Optical illusions trick us into thinking that we are seeing something different than what is actually there for us to see. Optical illusions occur because our brain perceives an image in a particular way.

Optical illusions are all around us. They occur in the natural world. A familiar illusion on a hot summer day is called a mirage. When driving along a hot road, sometimes our eyes seem to think that there is water on the road in front of us. As we approach that spot, we realize it was just an illusion. This happens because the heat from the road is rising and light from the sun hits it in a way that makes our eyes think there's water ahead.

Some animals and insects use illusions. Lions blend into the long brown grasses around them. This keeps them hidden from their soon-to-be meals. Insects such as the walking stick use an illusion to keep from being eaten. The walking stick looks like its name suggests—a stick!

Besides natural illusions, there are many human-made illusions too. Sometimes people call these brainteasers. Pictures are created to show different things at different times. Sometimes people don't see the same things in the same picture. One example of this is a picture that shows the word *ME*. When that same picture is looked at a bit differently, you may see the word YOU in it too.

Optical illusions are not only fun to look for but they have uses in nature. Keep your eyes open, but remember that you can't always believe what you see!

Sleuth Work

Gather Evidence Write three details that tell about optical illusions in nature.

Ask Questions Write two questions that you have about optical illusions for which you could research answers.

Make Your Case There is an expression that says, "seeing is believing." Do you think it is true more often than it is not true? Write a paragraph that states your opinion.

Becoming an ANIMAL EXPERT

Do you like animals? Are you curious about why they do the things they do? If you answered "Yes" to these questions, you might make a good scientist some day.

There are many scientists who specialize in the study of animal behavior. These scientists go by many names: doctor, curator, researcher, trainer, zoologist, biologist, and veterinarian, just to name a few.

To become an animal behavior scientist, you must go to college to learn as much as you can about animals. In fact, most animal behavior jobs require advanced degrees, which means you may have to go to college for more than the usual four years. Becoming an animal behavior specialist takes a lot of studying, hard work, and good grades.

When you're done with your studies, you might become a professor at a college. Here you might teach classes, research animals, and write articles explaining what you've discovered about these animals.

You might become a veterinarian, or animal doctor. Vets take care of many different kinds of animals. You might even go to work for a company that makes products for animals, such as food or medicine.

Other animal behavior specialists go to work at zoos, aquariums, or nature preserves. They figure out the best ways to care for and study the animals that live there.

Take a look at some famous animal behavior specialists. Charles Darwin (1809–1882) was a scientist who became famous for his study of how animals evolve, or change over time. Rachel Carson (1907–1964) was a well-known American ecologist and marine biologist. Jane Goodall (1934–) is a famous animal behavior scientist. She is best known for her study of chimpanzees in Africa. Steve Irwin (1962–2006) was another well-known animal expert. He ran a zoo in Australia and was famous for his knowledge of crocodiles. These scientists understood and continue to understand that all living creatures are linked together on our planet.

All around the world—in oceans, jungles, deserts, and labs—scientists like these are making new discoveries about all kinds of animals. Maybe someday you will be one of them too!

SLEUTH WORK

Gather Evidence What skills and training are needed to study and work with animals? Write down evidence to support your answer.

Make Your Case Do you think you would make a good animal behavior scientist someday? Write at least five sentences that support your opinion.

Ask Questions Working with a partner, take turns interviewing each other for a job that requires working with animals. What questions would you ask?

Recognizing the
NAVAJO CODE TALKERS

On July 26, 2001, four Native Americans received the highest civilian award that the U.S. Congress can give—the Congressional Gold Medal. Inside the Capitol in Washington, D.C., President George W. Bush addressed the audience. He said, "Today, America honors twenty one Native Americans who, in a desperate hour, gave their country a service only they could give. In war, using their native language, they relayed secret messages that turned the course of battle."

The four men standing beside the President were John Brown, Chester Nez, Lloyd Oliver, and Allen Dale June. A fifth man, Joe Palmer, was too sick to make the trip to the Capitol. These five men were the only survivors of the group of World War II Marines who served as Navajo Code Talkers.

It took about sixty years for these men to be recognized for their service. Soon after, however, they received even more acclaim. A toy company redesigned some of their action figures. They had them speak Diné code, a Navajo language. Four months after the ceremony, a member of the U.S. government traveled to Window Rock, Arizona, the capital of the Navajo nation. He presented silver medals to more than 100 Code Talkers. These men were survivors of a unit of 399 soldiers who had been trained by the original group of Code Talkers. Hollywood later released *Windtalkers*, a movie version of the story.

Code Talker Bill Toledo received a silver medal. He was recruited to the Marines from high school. He was a Code Talker for three years, from October 1942 to October 1945. Toledo served in many battles and faced incredible danger. On the island of Guam, he barely missed being hit by sniper bullets. Thanks to his quick feet, he escaped unharmed. Later, while marching through the jungle, he was mistaken for a Japanese soldier. He was taken prisoner at gunpoint. Once the mistake was realized, he was given a bodyguard so it would not happen again.

Toledo says it's important to share his experiences with younger generations. He wants them to understand freedom comes at a cost. He wants them to appreciate the sacrifices made so that Americans can enjoy their freedom.

SLEUTH WORK

Gather Evidence How does the author feel about the Code Talkers? Write down evidence from the article to support this.

Ask Questions If you could talk to a Code Talker about his experiences, what would you ask him? Write down two factual and two opinion questions that you would ask.

Make Your Case Given the technology we have now, do you think a Code Talker would be as useful in the military today? Write a paragraph that supports your opinion.

Learning a New Language

There was a buzz in the classroom. Mrs. Taylor announced that a new student was joining the class soon, and the student was coming from Mexico.

After the announcement, Mrs. Taylor asked everyone to quiet down. "I know you're excited about our new student," she said, "but I have some other good news too."

"Our principal, Mrs. Littlefield, and I have decided that it'd be helpful for us to learn some Spanish. That'll help us communicate better with Alita. She can learn English while we learn Spanish," Mrs. Taylor explained.

Mrs. Taylor's class broke out in cheers of excitement.

"I know some Spanish already," informed Kelly. "My grandparents speak Spanish."

"Great!" Mrs. Taylor responded. "You can help us learn Spanish too. We have a guest coming today who's a Spanish tutor. He's going to teach us some Spanish language basics. Then you'll feel more confident talking with Alita when she comes."

Just then a man walked in and introduced himself. "Hello, or *hola!* I'm Señor Alvarez, and I'll be working with you over the next few weeks. Before you know it, you'll be able to have a simple conversation with Alita."

Señor Alvarez began the first lesson. "There are a few tips that I'd like to share with you. Remember these, and you'll have an easier time learning a new language.

"First, you'll want to spend as much time as you can listening to the language, so I'll leave some Spanish language CDs for you. Listen to these and practice saying the words with the speaker.

"The second tip is to spend time every day studying. I'll be here twice a week, and when I'm not here, work together in a small group and practice what you have learned.

"The third, and maybe the most important tip, is not to worry about making mistakes. Sometimes you make mistakes even when you're speaking English, so don't worry about making mistakes when you're trying to learn how to speak Spanish. Don't be afraid to ask me or Alita, when she arrives, how to say or pronounce something."

Señor Alvarez then taught the class how to say a few words and phrases in Spanish. After the tutoring session ended, many students were eager to practice. They followed Señor Alvarez's first tip: they grabbed the Spanish language CDs that he left for them. They had no time to lose. The students were excited about being able to greet Alita in Spanish when she arrived!

Sleuth Work

Gather Evidence Why does Mrs. Taylor feel it is important for her class to learn Spanish? Write evidence from the story.

Ask Questions Write several questions that you might ask Alita about her home and life in Mexico.

Make Your Case Should schools require students to learn another language? Explain your answer using evidence from the text and any personal experiences.

August 24

Dear Red Fox,

If you are reading this, you have successfully cracked my code. Good work, agent!

My parents just picked me up from summer camp. They couldn't wait to hear about the arts and crafts and campfire songs I learned.

However, only you know what I *really* did at camp this summer. The spy tools I learned about will help me on my next mission. Read on for more information.

Did you know that people used to hide messages in paintings and drawings? That's called steganography. Now we can encrypt messages and hide them inside digital files. Be sure to take lots of photos at your cousin's birthday party next weekend! We can use the image files to hide messages.

I got a new tip on using secret codes, or ciphers, too. Instead of having to think of new ciphers all the time, we can use our computers to do the hard work. The codes that computers create are much harder to crack.

I can't wait to use these new tools so we can communicate in secret next week at the middle school orientation. Do you want to join me on this mission? Just to be on the safe side, we should scope out a good dead drop at school. (Spies *always* use dead drops!) Let's look for a place in an area that is usually crowded so that we can blend in and access the dead drop unnoticed. We can send text messages to keep track of each other, but it's good to have a backup plan in case of technological difficulties.

I can't wait to learn the moves you mastered at martial arts camp. See you next week!

Agent Campfire

SLEUTH WORK

Gather Evidence What spy tools are discussed in the letter? Write one detail about each tool.

Ask Questions Write two interesting questions you would like to have answered about one of the spy tools discussed in the letter. Where could you find the answers to these questions?

Make Your Case A dead drop is a secret place that is usually in plain sight. Where in your classroom or school would make the best dead drop? List reasons to support your answer.

Unit 5
Adventures by Land, Air, and Water

Hello, Sleuthhounds!

In this unit, you will be looking for clues about some adventures. Here are some sleuth tips to help you. You're on the right track!

Sleuth Tips

Gather Evidence

How do sleuths find clues given by authors?

- Sleuths look for hints in what they read. They look for words that show opinions.
- Sleuths pay close attention as they read and reread. They watch for evidence of sequence or cause and effect.

Ask Questions

Where do sleuths get answers to their questions?

- Sleuths look back at the text and images for answers. They also discuss ideas and possible answers with others.
- Sleuths use other resources such as computers and books. They also know it may take a long time to find answers.

Make Your Case

How do sleuths use evidence when they make a case?

- Sleuths use evidence to explain their thinking. They tell how the evidence led them to their conclusion.
- Sleuths use evidence from the text and images. Citing where the evidence was found can be very helpful.

Prove It!

Why do sleuths think about who will read what they write?

- Sleuths choose the style of writing that fits best. They always try to explain their thinking clearly and completely.
- Sleuths use many different approaches. Sometimes a sleuth writes a story. Sometimes a report or diagram works better.

ARE YOU PREPARED FOR AN EMERGENCY?

It is important to be prepared for emergencies. You never know when they may strike. In school, you prepare for emergencies by practicing drills in case of a fire, tornado, or hurricane. However, do you practice being ready for emergencies at home?

One of the most important things you can do to be prepared for an emergency is to put together an emergency kit. This kit should always be kept in a place at home that is easy to remember and find. Once a disaster hits, the emergency kit should supply you with everything you need.

An emergency kit includes basic supplies that will help your family survive if there is no electricity or water or if you are unable to leave your home for as long as 72 hours. When a disaster hits, it can take days before rescue workers reach you, especially if you are stranded in your home. Therefore, it is important to pack supplies in the emergency kit that will allow you to survive without outside help for several days.

One of the most important supplies in an emergency kit is water. It is important to have one gallon of water per person in your family for at least three days. That means that you should have three gallons of water put aside just for you! You should also have three days' worth of food. Food needs to be nonperishable, or food that cannot spoil. Foods like granola bars, canned tuna, dried fruits, and peanut butter are foods that won't spoil for a long time.

A radio that can be powered by batteries is also important. If there is no electricity, the only way to know what is happening is to listen to a radio that is powered by batteries. Be sure to have extra batteries in your emergency supply kit too. Flashlights, a whistle to signal for help, and a first-aid kit are also very important to include among your emergency supplies.

Once you create your emergency supply kit, be sure to check your food and water supplies every six months. You may want to replace them then to have fresh food and water on hand.

During an emergency, always remember to remain calm. Knowing that you have planned ahead and are prepared can be very reassuring.

SLEUTH WORK

Gather Evidence Make a list of items that you would include in your emergency supply kit. Refer to the text for clues as to what you should include.

Ask Questions The Red Cross helps many communities when a disaster strikes. Write three questions you would ask a Red Cross volunteer about preparing for an emergency.

Make Your Case How would you persuade someone to prepare for an emergency? Think about the reason a person may not have an emergency plan yet. Write a paragraph that includes both facts and opinions.

AN AMAZING DISCOVERY

"Marcus, get your mother!" Aldo yelled. "I have something to show her!" It was a sizzling hot day. Aldo had risen early so he and his son could work in the coolness of the morning. They raised olives and grapes on a quaint farm in Italy in the early 1700s. These crops flourished in the fertile soil, made rich by volcanic ash.

That morning Aldo was digging a new well. As he was digging, his shovel hit something hard. He put the shovel down and started scraping at the dirt with his hands. When Marcus returned with his mother, Gina, they found Aldo looking into the eyes of a beautiful face. They helped him continue digging until they had uncovered an entire statue carved from marble.

"Aldo, my sister told me about a neighbor who found something like this when he dug his well," Gina said. "Do you think this is part of the same collection of ruins?"

The family met with their neighbors. Soon everyone was comparing items they had found in their own farm fields. People had unearthed coins, jewelry, bowls, and bricks. Some had even found bones.

Aldo and his neighbors worked their lands, and uncovered many other interesting artifacts buried in the soil. Soon, however, they were told to stop. They found out their farms were located near where the ancient city of Herculaneum had once been. To continue digging might damage the ruins and make it impossible to learn their secrets from the past.

Many centuries earlier, Herculaneum and Pompeii had been thriving cities. Yet one horrific day in A.D. 79, they were destroyed by a volcanic eruption. That day the nearby volcano known as Mount Vesuvius (ve SUE vee es) erupted. It buried the cities of Herculaneum and Pompeii under rock and ash. Thousands of people died, and everything in the cities was burned or buried.

Since the discovery of ruins that remain from the two cities, historians and archaeologists from all over the world have come to the area to excavate and see what else they can find. Today tourists flock to Pompeii and Herculaneum to see the ruins.

Aldo and his neighbors often talked about what life must have been like in Herculaneum. They thought about how, if they had lived in the first century A.D., their farms would have been right in the middle of the city. Certainly they were glad to have lived instead at a different time, when their farms became a popular tourist attraction that drew visitors from around the world.

SLEUTH WORK

Gather Evidence What evidence helps you understand that this is historical fiction? List three details.

Ask Questions Write three interesting questions about Pompeii.

Make Your Case Do you think historical artifacts should belong to the person who finds them or be owned by a museum and displayed for more people to see? Give two reasons to support your opinion.

GRANDMA'S HERO

"Grandma, I'm home!" Denzel slammed the door behind him, dropped his heavy backpack on the couch, and headed straight for the kitchen, as he always did after school.

"Grandma?" Denzel called, surprised she wasn't standing in the kitchen preparing dinner. "She must be upstairs," he reasoned, so he shrugged his shoulders, grabbed an apple, and headed to the family room to do his homework.

After taking a few bites of his apple, Denzel started feeling a little uneasy. It wasn't like his grandmother not to say hello when he came home. *Where is she,* he thought to himself.

He decided to check upstairs for her. Her door was halfway open, so he quietly knocked and pushed it open. "Grandma?" Denzel said softly. "Grandma!" Denzel shouted with panic in his voice.

Denzel noticed his grandmother lying on the floor next to her bed. In no time, he bolted to her side to check on her.

Just weeks before, a paramedic had visited Denzel's health class at school, and he had talked about what to do in case of an emergency just like this one. Denzel remembered what he had learned and jumped into action, prodding Grandma and asking, "Grandma, are you OK?" When his grandmother did not respond, Denzel ran to the phone and called 9-1-1.

A dispatcher answered, and Denzel frantically explained the situation.

The dispatcher calmed Denzel and asked him to stay on the line while he waited for the paramedics to arrive. As they waited, the dispatcher gave Denzel some instructions. First, she asked Denzel if his grandmother was breathing. Denzel said he could not tell for sure. The dispatcher then explained to him how he might have to perform CPR. Thankfully, a paramedic had taught his class how to do CPR during the class visit.

The paramedics arrived quicker than Denzel had expected, and they began taking care of his grandmother. Soon she was awake and responding to their questions. The paramedics told Denzel they thought she would be fine, but they would take her to the hospital to be certain.

One of the paramedics pulled Denzel aside. "Your grandma is very lucky to have you," she said. "You are a hero."

Denzel felt even luckier that Grandma was going to be fine. Denzel was the proudest he'd ever been, but he didn't really feel like a hero. He just did what he needed to do.

SLEUTH WORK

Gather Evidence Write down evidence from the story that shows how Denzel feels about his grandma.

Ask Questions Write three questions that you might ask someone who was a "hero" during an emergency.

Make Your Case Who is the greatest American hero? Make a case for the hero you have chosen and provide three reasons for your choice.

A MAN OF PERSISTENCE

Explorer Sir Ernest Shackleton might be the most persistent man who ever lived. On December 5, 1914, he and twenty-seven men set out on a ship called *Endurance*. They hoped to reach the Antarctic continent and become the first people to cross the land on foot.

Despite the predictions of a terrible winter, *Endurance* left South Georgia Island, a remote island in the southern Atlantic Ocean. It headed for Vahsel Bay on Antarctica. Just two days later, the vessel ran into pack ice. For the next six weeks, the ship wove through ice floes.

On January 18, 1915, one day short of landing, the ship hit another thick pack ice. By the next morning, ice had enclosed the ship. Shackleton soon realized the ship was securely stuck in the ice and would remain stuck through many long winter months. During this time, Shackleton had his crew stick to their routines and exercise the sled dogs they had brought with them.

Ten months later, the crew still remained on board. In October 1915, pressure from the ice began to damage the ship, and it began slowly sinking. Shackleton and his crew abandoned the ship and made camp on the surrounding ice. On November 21, 1915, *Endurance* sank completely.

The crew camped on the ice for several months, and in April 1916, the ice floe broke in half, causing the crew to flee in

December 5, 1914	January 18, 1915	October 1915	November 21, 191
Endurance sets sail.	*Endurance* stranded in ice.	Crew abandons ship.	*Endurance* sinks.

lifeboats. Days later, they landed on Elephant Island, about 350 miles from where the *Endurance* sank.

Shackleton knew he had to take a drastic step if they were ever to be rescued. Elephant Island was too remote for a rescue attempt. So a group of six men set off in a lifeboat for South Georgia Island, where their journey had begun.

The lifeboat landed on the west side of South Georgia Island in May 1916. The whaling stations—the only source of rescue—were on the east side. Shackleton and two others left on foot to travel the twenty-two miles to the nearest stations.

Within thirty-six hours, the men had made it to a whaling station and began planning the crew's rescue. Finally, on August 30, 1916, the crew was rescued from Elephant Island. After almost two years, the ordeal was over, and not one crew member had died. It was an amazing expedition with a happy ending because of one man's persistence to bring everyone home.

SLEUTH WORK

Gather Evidence Shackleton was a persistent man. Write three details from the text that support this statement.

Ask Questions If you could talk to Sir Shackleton about the decisions he made, what three questions would you ask?

Make Your Case Which part of the expedition of the *Endurance* do you think would have been the most difficult? Support your opinion with evidence from the text.

April 1916	**May 1916**	**August 30, 1916**
Crew flees in lifeboats. Some settle on Elephant Island. Others head to South Georgia Island to get help.	Small crew lands on South Georgia Island.	All crew members rescued from Elephant Island.

Lunar Vehicles

How would you travel across Earth if there were no roads, railways, or bridges? You could go on foot, but there would be challenges, especially when trying to cross rough or mountainous terrain. Astronauts on the moon face this problem. There are no public transportation or highway systems on the moon. More importantly, the surface of the Moon is rocky and full of craters—some deeper than others.

In the early 1970s, NASA (National Aeronautics and Space Administration) sent astronauts on three missions, *Apollo 15, 16,* and *17,* to explore the surface of the moon with a four-wheeled, open-air buggy called a Lunar Roving Vehicle (LRV). The LRV was battery powered and held two passengers. It was built to withstand the extreme environment on the moon, where temperatures can get very hot or very cold in a matter of seconds. The LRV was equipped with a video camera and an antenna that looked like an umbrella. This enabled astronauts to send pictures and sounds from the moon back to Earth.

Four LRVs were built: three were used on missions, and one was used for spare parts. Each LRV was used for three excursions. These trips let astronauts explore the moon and travel farther and longer than they had on foot. The LRV could climb steep, rocky slopes and move easily over the moon's surface. It was able to carry more than twice its weight. This allowed astronauts to bring equipment with them as well as collect rocks. The LRV was not designed to be used for a long time and each vehicle was only used on one mission.

At the turn of the twenty-first century, NASA began developing models for a modern vehicle. One model is called the Lunar Electric Rover. Unlike LRVs, the Lunar Electric Rover is pressurized and has twelve wheels. Additionally, it can be used for ten years rather than just one mission. Like its predecessor, it can carry only two astronauts. However, the astronauts can sleep and use sanitary facilities in the Lunar Electric Rover. These features would allow astronauts to travel thousands of miles on excursions lasting up to fourteen days.

Unfortunately, the technology needed to put a Lunar Electric Rover on the moon is not yet available. In 2020, NASA plans to send astronauts back to the moon. Perhaps a Lunar Electric Rover will be their "wheels" on the moon.

Sleuth Work

Gather Evidence How is a Lunar Electric Rover different from a Lunar Roving Vehicle? Provide at least two pieces of evidence from the text.

Ask Questions Write two questions that you have about the Lunar Electric Rover. Note sources where you might find answers to your questions.

Make Your Case Do you feel it is a good use of money and time to send astronauts back to the moon? State reasons to support your opinion.

Unit 6
Reaching for Goals

Calling all Sleuthhounds!

In this unit, you will be looking for clues about what it takes to achieve goals. Here are some sleuth tips to help you. Keep it up!

Sleuth Tips

Gather Evidence

How do sleuths know if evidence is important?

- Sleuths find and record lots of evidence. They don't always know what evidence will prove to be the most important.
- Sleuths look for evidence that connects information and addresses the questions.

Ask Questions

How do sleuths think of interesting questions to ask?

- Sleuths might base a question on what interests them the most. They know others may wonder about the same thing.
- Sleuths think about what is missing from the information they have been given.

Make Your Case

How do sleuths learn from other sleuths?

- Sleuths are good listeners. They listen to see what evidence they may have overlooked.
- Sleuths ask questions to see how others put the evidence together in different ways.

Prove It!

How do sleuths prepare to share what they know?

- Sleuths reread what they have written. They are willing to make changes to make their ideas clearer.
- Sleuths practice. Practice can make sharing less stressful and more fun.

FOUR SCORE AND SEVEN YEARS AGO

"Four score and seven years ago" are the words that begin a short speech by President Abraham Lincoln. This speech has become one of the most famous speeches in our country's history. President Lincoln delivered this speech on November 19, 1863, in Gettysburg, Pennsylvania. This speech, known as the Gettysburg Address, followed one of the bloodiest battles in our country's history.

From July 1 to July 3, 1863, the town of Gettysburg, Pennsylvania, was the site of conflict and war. In those three days, more than 51,000 soldiers were wounded, killed, or went missing in this Civil War battle. In the following days, the people of Gettysburg cared for wounded and dead soldiers. They welcomed soldiers' families and rebuilt damaged homes and barns.

Just four months later, the people of Gettysburg opened their arms again. They welcomed thousands of people to be a part of the dedication ceremony for the new soldiers' cemetery.

On November 19, 1863, famous speaker Edward Everett spoke for two hours to thousands of people. He talked about the heroism of the soldiers. He talked about his belief that the North and South would reunite. He believed our country would become even stronger.

After Everett's two-hour speech, President Lincoln spoke for just three minutes. He reminded the crowd that the nation was built on the belief that all men are created equal. He believed that the cemetery gave a final resting place for all those who had died fighting for the country. He shared that it was now the country's choice to either give in to failure or be even more devoted to freedom. He wanted our country's government to persist in the belief that the government was "of the people, by the people, for the people."

Lincoln's Gettysburg Address marks an important turning point in our country's history. Benjamin French, who helped plan the dedication ceremony at Gettysburg, saw the effect President Lincoln's speech had on the audience. He wrote in his diary: "It was the spontaneous outburst of heartfelt confidence in *their own* President." The country would reunite and become stronger than it had been before.

SLEUTH WORK

Gather Evidence Make a list of ways the people of Gettysburg came together during such a difficult time in our country's history.

Ask Questions Write two questions you would ask a historian about President Lincoln's Gettysburg Address.

Make Your Case Do you think it is easier or more difficult today for a speech to make a difference in the nation than it was during the time that Lincoln lived? Write your opinion and include at least three convincing reasons.

Living with Asthma

If you have asthma, you might find yourself suddenly coughing, wheezing, and struggling to take a breath. Asthma makes the muscles in your airways contract so tightly that it is hard for air to get into your lungs. It also makes your body produce thick mucus in your airways, which can make it hard to breathe.

Asthma attacks usually start with coughing and a tight feeling in your chest. An attack can last a half hour to several hours. Some people have asthma attacks often. Others suffer from them only a few times a year. Today, asthma can be treated using medicine delivered through inhalers or by other methods.

If you have asthma, you are not alone. Many famous artists, scientists, musicians, and entertainers have asthma. Olympic athletes Kristi Yamaguchi and Jackie Joyner-Kersee have lived with asthma, as have U.S. Presidents Theodore Roosevelt, Woodrow Wilson, John F. Kennedy, and William (Bill) Clinton.

Theodore Roosevelt was often sick and very weak as a child because of his bad asthma. Back then, there were no